I0814879

JAPANESE MYTHOLOGY

Hachiman

BY HEATHER C. HUDAK

CONTENT CONSULTANT
MARJORIE BURGE, PhD
ASSISTANT PROFESSOR OF JAPANESE
UNIVERSITY OF COLORADO BOULDER

Kids Core
An Imprint of Abdo Publishing
abdobooks.com

abdobooks.com

Published by Abdo Publishing, a division of ABDO, PO Box 398166, Minneapolis, Minnesota 55439.

Printed in the United States of America, North Mankato, Minnesota.
102024
012025

Cover Photo: Shutterstock Images
Interior Photos: Pictures From History/CPA Media Pte Ltd/Alamy, 4–5; Universal History Archive/Universal Images Group/Getty Images, 7; Print Collector/Hulton Fine Art Collection/Getty Images, 8; Lebrecht Music & Arts/Alamy, 10–11; Pictures From History/Universal Images Group/Getty Images, 12, 28 (bottom); Pictures from History/Bridgeman Images, 14, 29 (top); Shim Harno/Alamy, 16; John S. Lander/LightRocket/Getty Images, 18–19, 28 (top); NPL-DeA Picture Library/Bridgeman Images, 21; Shutterstock Images, 22, 29 (bottom); Arif Iqball Photography-Japan/Alamy, 23; yuki5287/Flickr, 24; Red Line Editorial, 25; The History Collection/Alamy, 26

Editor: Christa Kelly
Series Designer: Ryan Gale

Library of Congress Control Number: 2024938349

Publisher's Cataloging-in-Publication Data

Names: Hudak, Heather C., author.
Title: Hachiman / by Heather C. Hudak
Description: Minneapolis, Minnesota: ABDO Publishing, 2025 | Series: Japanese mythology | Includes online resources and index.
Identifiers: ISBN 9781098295967 (lib. bdg.) | ISBN 9798384916963 (ebook)
Subjects: LCSH: Mythology, Japanese--Juvenile literature. | Deities--Juvenile literature. | Hachiman (Shinto deity)--Juvenile literature. | Hachiman Daibosatsu (Shinto deity)--Juvenile literature. | Mythology, Asian--Juvenile literature.
Classification: DDC 398.21--dc23

CONTENTS

Kublai Khan ruled the Mongol Empire from 1260 to 1294 CE.

The Mongol Invasion

Kublai Khan (pronounced KOOB-lye KAHN) was a skilled warrior and military leader. In 1260 CE, he became the **emperor** of the Mongol Empire. This empire started in present-day Mongolia. Over time, it stretched across Asia.

Kublai wanted to bring China under his rule. He took the country by force. He also brought Korea under his rule. Kublai then set his sights on Japan. He sent several letters to the emperor of Japan. He demanded that the emperor surrender to the Mongols. The emperor never responded. This angered Kublai. He decided to invade Japan.

In 1274, Kublai sent about 40,000 men and 900 ships to raid Japan. Japan's warriors, the

Samurai

Samurai were Japanese warriors. The first samurai date back to the 1100s CE. They rode horses. They fought with swords and bows. From 1185 to 1868, the samurai were among Japan's most powerful groups.

In Japan, a divine wind sent by the gods is known as a *kamikaze*.

samurai, were not prepared for such a huge battle. The Japanese people prayed to the gods for help. Hachiman, the god of war, did not let them down. He and the other gods sent **divine** winds across the waters. The winds stirred up a massive storm. The storm destroyed about one-third of the Mongolian fleet. About 13,000 men drowned.

After Kublai's ships were destroyed, Japan's warriors were able to defeat the rest of the enemy troops in battle.

But Kublai refused to give up. In 1281, he put together one of the largest battle fleets the world had ever seen. He sent about 140,000 men and 4,400 ships to Japan. Again, the Japanese people prayed to the gods for help. Hachiman and the other gods listened. A massive storm struck the Mongolian fleet. At least half the men drowned. Only a few hundred ships remained. Japan was safe once again.

Hachiman and Shinto

Shinto is a Japanese religion. The word *Shinto* means "the way of the gods." Shinto centers around *kami*, or "spirits." Many gods are kami. Hachiman is one of the most well-known Shinto kami.

Mythology is an important part of Shinto. Myths are stories. Many Japanese myths are about gods and heroes. Some tell the story of Hachiman.

Explore Online

Visit the website below. Does it give any new information about samurai that wasn't in Chapter One?

Samurai

abdocorelibrary.com/hachiman

In some stories, Emperor Chuai, *left*, died immediately after he disobeyed the kami. In other stories, he died in battle soon after.

The God of War

According to Japanese myths, Chuai (choo-eye) was an early emperor of Japan. But his reign was cut short. A powerful kami told him to invade Korea. Chuai did not obey. He died soon after as a punishment for not listening to the kami.

In art, Jingu is often shown with a sword or a bow and arrows.

Emperor Chuai's wife took control of the country. Today she is known as Jingu. She was pregnant with Chuai's child. She tied a stone to her belly to stop herself from giving birth. Then, Jingu decided to obey the kami and invade Korea. She led Japan's troops into battle.

Jingu was a talented leader. She spoke with kami and listened to their advice. The kami also kept her safe during battles. With their help, Jingu's troops quickly won the war. When she returned to Japan, she gave birth to a son. As he was born, eight banners came down from the heavens. It was a sign that her baby would be a divine emperor. Jingu named the child Homuda. Today, he is known as Ojin.

Emperor Ojin

According to Japanese myths, Emperor Ojin was the fifteenth emperor of Japan. Though historians are not sure if he really existed, Ojin is an important figure in Japan. He is honored with a massive grave known as a mausoleum.

Ojin ruled Japan from 270 to 310 CE.

Avatars of Hachiman

Over the years, people in Japan began to link Jingu and Ojin to Hachiman, the god of war.

They decided that Jingu and Ojin had been avatars for Hachiman. This means that they were the god in human form.

By about 840 CE, Ojin and Hachiman became known as the same being. The god quickly grew more popular. Around 1046, Hachiman became the **patron deity** of the Minamoto clan. The clan would play an important role in the Japanese government. They chose Hachiman to be their deity because they were warriors.

Yorinobu was a powerful member of the Minamoto clan. He claimed Hachiman was his **ancestor**. Yorinobu's son Yoriyoshi said Hachiman helped him win a war. Yoriyoshi built a **shrine** to honor Hachiman.

Yoshiie was a fierce samurai, a talented poet, and a powerful leader.

Later, Yoriyoshi had a son named Yoshiie. Yoshiie was a skilled warrior. He became known as Hachiman Taro, or First Son of Hachiman. Some people believed he was an avatar for Hachiman.

Primary Source

An ancient Japanese book called *Kojiki* explains how a kami told Chuai to take over Korea:

> Westward lies a land rich in gold, silver, and all manner of marvelous treasures that dazzle the eye. I now give you this land.

When Chuai refused, the kami angrily said:

> No longer will you rule over all under heaven as your **realm**!

Source: Ō no Yasumaro. Translated by Gustav Heldt. *The Kojiki: An Account of Ancient Matters.* Columbia University Press, 2014.

Comparing Texts

Read the quote. Does it support the information in this book? Or does it give a new perspective?

Hachiman appears in kagura, Shinto dances that honor kami and tell stories.

CHAPTER 3

Honoring Hachiman

Today, Hachiman is one of the most popular Shinto kami. He is often shown in art. He sometimes carries a bow and arrows to show he was a skilled archer. Other times, Hachiman is depicted as a dove. This bird was his messenger.

Hachiman is also shown as other people. Sometimes he is shown as a Buddhist **monk**. Other times he appears as Emperor Ojin.

Shrines

Hachiman is honored at shrines. There are as many as 44,000 shrines dedicated to Hachiman across Japan. Usa Shrine on Kyushu Island is the most important Hachiman shrine. It was built around 725 CE.

Hachiman in Buddhism

Buddhism is a religion from India. Hachiman is an important god in Japanese Buddhism. He was the first Japanese god to be given the Buddhist title *Daibosatsu*. This title means "Great Buddha-to-be." Hachiman is known as the protector of Buddhist temples.

The *Tōdai-ji Hachiman* sculpture was carved in 1201 CE. It shows Hachiman as a Buddhist monk.

Before entering Iwashimizu Hachimangū, visitors should wash their hands and mouths. This practice is common at many Shinto shrines.

In 859, a monk said that Hachiman had spoken to him. The god promised to go to Mount Otokoyama and protect Japan. The Iwashimizu Hachimangū shrine was built for Hachiman on

During festivals at Tsurugaoka Hachimangu, performers show off their archery skills on horseback.

top of the mountain. Many members of Japan's **imperial** family have worshiped at the shrine in the hundreds of years since it was built.

Tsurugaoka Hachimangu shrine was built in 1063. Minamoto Yoriyoshi built the shrine to thank Hachiman for helping him win a battle. In 1180, the shrine was expanded and moved to its current site in Kamakura.

The trees at Umi Hachimangu are sacred. They are said to be 2,000 years old.

Umi Hachimangu is another important shrine. It is located in a town called Umi on Kyushu Island. This shrine marks the place where Jingu gave birth to Ojin.

Protecting Children

Hachiman is often considered a protector of pregnancy and childbirth. He is also thought

Hachiman Shrines

Hachiman shrines are located all around Japan.

to be a guardian of children. Pregnant women come to Umi Hachimangu to ask Hachiman to protect their unborn children.

Today, Jingu, *center*, Ojin, and Hachiman are important figures in Japan.

Women also write prayers to Hachiman on stones. The prayers ask Hachiman to protect them during childbirth. This practice comes from the way Jingu used a stone to delay giving birth to Ojin.

Hachiman is one of Shinto's most important kami. Hundreds of years after he helped wash away the Mongol forces, he continues to protect the country. Today, he is an important part of Japanese culture.

Further Evidence

Look at the website below. Does it give any new evidence to support Chapter Three?

Shrines

abdocorelibrary.com/hachiman

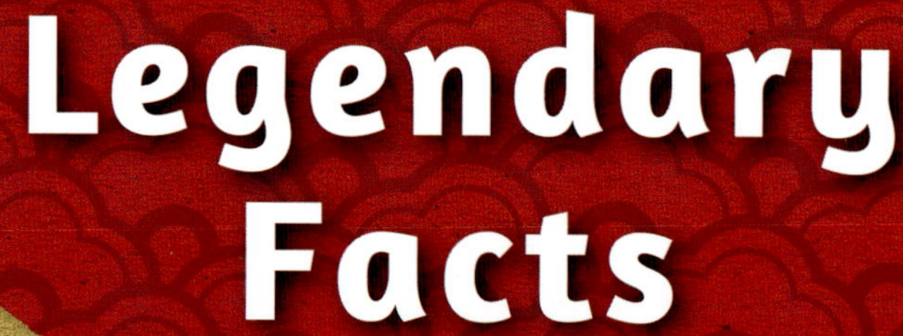

Legendary Facts

Hachiman is the Shinto god of war.

Jingu and Emperor Ojin were avatars of Hachiman.

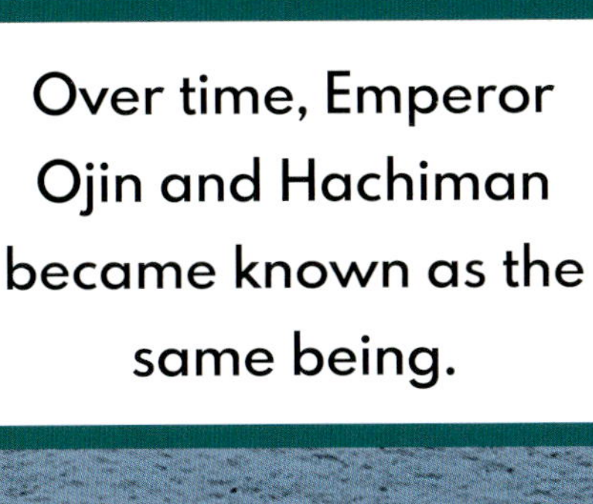

Over time, Emperor Ojin and Hachiman became known as the same being.

Today, art and shrines honor Hachiman.

Glossary

ancestor
a person from whom someone is descended

divine
relating to or coming from a god

emperor
the ruler of an empire

imperial
relating to an emperor or empire

monk
a person who has taken religious vows and devotes their life to prayer

patron deity
a god worshipped as a supporting figure for a group

realm
a place that a person controls, such as a kingdom or empire

shrine
a place where gods and other religious figures are honored and worshipped

Online Resources

To learn more about Hachiman and Japanese mythology, visit our free resource websites below.

Visit **abdocorelibrary.com** or scan this QR code for free Common Core resources for teachers and students, including vetted activities, multimedia, and booklinks, for deeper subject comprehension.

Visit **abdobooklinks.com** or scan this QR code for free additional online weblinks for further learning. These links are routinely monitored and updated to provide the most current information available.

Learn More

Lee, Jean Kuo. *Tengu*. Abdo, 2025.

Van, R. L. *Japan*. Abdo, 2023.

Yasuda, Yuri. *Japanese Myths, Legends & Folktales: Bilingual English and Japanese Edition*. Tuttle, 2019.

Index

About the Author

Heather C. Hudak has written and edited hundreds of children's books. She writes about all kinds of topics, from animals to ancient legends. When Heather is not writing, she loves to travel. Japan was the sixtieth country she visited.